Don't be AFRAID

Win with AI

AF722550

Ameer Deen

Index

Dedication

This book is lovingly dedicated to my childhood friend, **Saravanan**.

Though you are no longer with us, your influence continues to shape my journey every day. You were the one who introduced me to the world of technology and inspired me to step into the IT field - a path that changed my life forever.

As I write these pages, I remember our friendship, your encouragement, and the belief you had in me. This book stands as a small tribute to the impact you had on my life.

Your presence may be gone, but your legacy lives in every achievement, every lesson, and every dream I continue to pursue.

Thank you, my friend.
This book is for you.

In loving memory of Saravanan.

Acknowledgement

My heartfelt gratitude goes to **Angeline**, my wife, whose steady encouragement and unwavering faith in my abilities inspired me to begin this writing journey. Her support through every challenge and her constant motivation have been invaluable in bringing this book to completion.

My heartfelt thanks also go to **my family members**, whose love, understanding, and continuous support have strengthened me throughout this process.

I would like to thank all the organizations that have been part of my professional journey for the opportunities, learning, and experiences they provided. Their support and contribution have played a significant role in shaping my career and making this book possible.

Finally, I extend my sincere appreciation to everyone who has been part of my journey, directly or indirectly, and whose support and encouragement have helped make this book possible.

Ameer Deen

1

AI Is Everywhere

"AI is not the future; it's the present."

Everywhere you turn, there is AI. Everywhere you look, people are talking about it. AI is no longer a futuristic concept - it has become part of our daily lives. (Whether we invited it or not!)

Many people think AI exists only in software or the technology industry. The truth is that AI has quietly become a part of how we live, work, learn, and communicate. From writing emails, creating presentations, and generating code to helping students learn, supporting doctors, and improving businesses, AI is transforming every industry.

Need proof? Think about these everyday activities:

- Morning Alarm and Sleep Tracking
- Weather Forecasts
- Google Maps and Traffic Navigation
- Social Media Feed Recommendations
- YouTube and Netflix Suggestions
- Google Search and Voice Search
- Siri, Alexa, and Google Assistant

- Customer Support Chatbots
- Facial Recognition and Phone Unlock
- Smart Home Automation
- Uber and Ola Ride-Hailing
- Smart Wearables and Fitness Tracking

Whether we realize it or not, AI has already become part of our smartphones, cars, offices, banks, hospitals, and homes.

The question is no longer, "**Should we use AI?**"

The real question is:

"**How can we use AI intelligently to improve our lives, careers, and future?**"

Before we answer that question, it is worth remembering that this is not the first time people have feared a new technology. When computers were introduced, many people thought they would replace jobs. Instead, they created millions of new opportunities. The same happened with the Internet; People believed it was unsafe and preferred doing things in person. Today, almost everything is online (It's amazing how quickly "I'll never use that" turns into "I can't live without it"). Just like computers and the Internet, AI will create new opportunities and transform the way we work.

Don't be afraid.
Win with it.

2
The AI Roadmap

As we discussed in the previous chapter, whenever an invention or technology is introduced, it is often accompanied by fear and uncertainty. That's completely normal.

"***The first step to overcoming fear is understanding.***"

Let's take some time to understand what AI really is. Stay with me for the next couple of chapters as we explore AI together. Once we understand how it works and what it can and cannot do, we can decide for ourselves whether it is something to fear - or something to embrace.

Many people think AI started with ChatGPT. Nope! If you look at the timeline, AI actually started back in our grandfathers' days. (Yes, AI is older than many of our dads!)

AI Roadmap: From Idea to Impact

1950 – The Idea Begins

- Alan Turing asks: "Can machines think?"

- The foundation of AI is born.

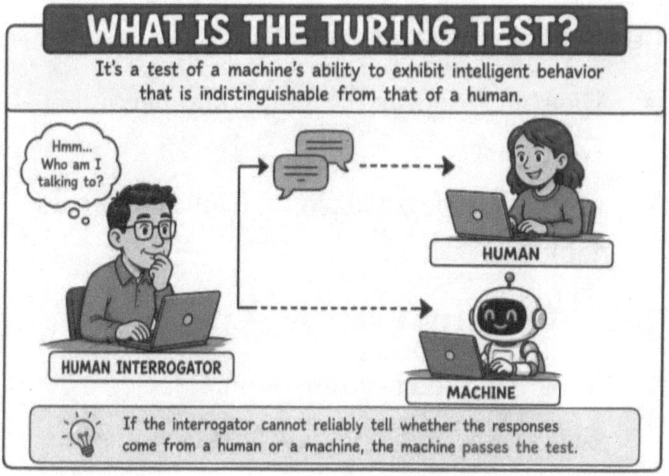

1956 – Birth of Artificial Intelligence

- The term "Artificial Intelligence" is officially introduced.
- AI becomes a field of study.

1960s–1980s – Early AI Research

- Rule-based systems emerge.
- AI learns to solve simple problems and play games.
- Limited by computing power.

1990s – Smarter Machines

- AI improves pattern recognition.

- 1997: IBM Deep Blue defeats world chess champion Garry Kasparov.

2000s – The Internet Era

- Massive amounts of digital data become available.
- AI systems begin learning from real-world data.

2010s – AI Enters Everyday Life

- Google Search becomes smarter.
- Siri, Alexa, and Google Assistant appear.
- Recommendation engines power YouTube, Netflix, and Amazon.
- AI has become part of daily life.

2020–2022 – Generative AI Revolution

- AI begins generating text, images, music, and code.
- ChatGPT brings AI into the mainstream.
- Millions start using AI personally and professionally.

2023–Today – AI Everywhere

- AI becomes part of everyday life and work.

- AI assistants help with writing, coding, learning, research, and creativity.
- Businesses rapidly adopt AI to improve productivity and efficiency.
- AI moves from being a tool for experts to a tool for everyone.

Now do you see how old AI really is?

And as we all know, older people usually make way for the younger generation (Trust me on this one !) - they don't come to disturb us. Instead, they share their knowledge, experience, advice, and support whenever we need it.

Think of AI the same way. It's here to assist us, guide us, and help us get things done more efficiently - not to compete with us.

Don't be afraid.
An experienced assistant.

3
Don't Fear - Understand AI

In the previous chapter, we discussed the AI roadmap and the journey ahead. Now, let us begin by understanding what Artificial Intelligence (AI) is, why it is important, and the various types of AI that exist today. (Trust me, it's much simpler than it sounds!)

Welcome to the world of AI.

AI (Artificial Intelligence) means making machines smart like humans. These machines can learn, think, understand, and make good decisions to help us. (*Think of AI as a super-smart assistant- one that works day and night, never complains, and thankfully never asks for a salary hike*!)

How AI works

1. Data – AI collects information from text, images, videos, and other sources.

2. Learning – AI learns patterns and relationships from the data.

3. Prediction – AI uses what it learned to make decisions or predictions.

4. Improvement – AI gets better over time with more data and feedback.

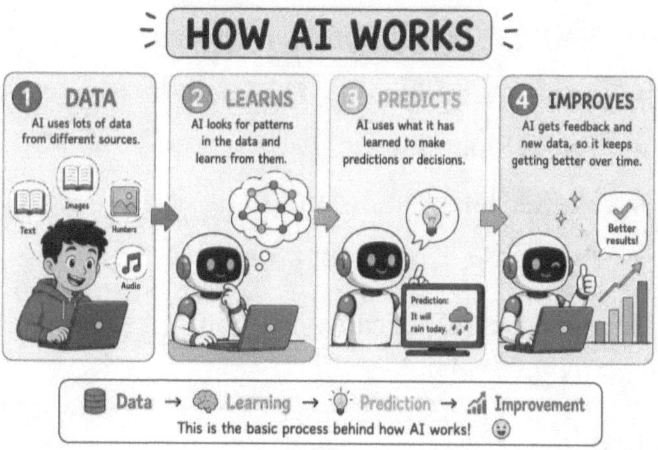

AI Evolution

1. Traditional AI: Follows predefined rules to make decisions.

Examples:

- Calculator
- ATM Machine
- Rule-based Chatbots
- Tax Calculation Software
- Chess Programs with predefined rules

2. Machine Learning (ML): Learns patterns from data and improves over time.

Examples:

- Netflix Movie Recommendations
- Amazon Product Recommendations
- Email Spam Filters
- Fraud Detection Systems
- Predictive Text Keyboards

3. Generative AI: Creates new content such as text, images, code, and videos.

Examples:

- ChatGPT
- Claude
- Gemini
- AI Image Generators

- AI Code Assistants

4. Agentic AI: AI that can plan, decide, and perform tasks to achieve a goal with minimal human intervention.

Examples:

- AI Research Agents
- AI Coding Agents
- Autonomous Customer Support Agents
- AI Personal Assistants that schedule meetings
- AI Workflow Automation Agents

5. AGI (Artificial General Intelligence): Thinks, learns, and solves problems like a human across any domain.

6. ASI (Artificial Super Intelligence): Surpasses human intelligence in all areas

---

Human Vs. AI

Don't worry when you see the heading 'Human vs AI.' It's not a battle - just a comparison. (If the heading sounds scary, we can always rename it!) 😀

~~Human Vs. AI~~

Humans + AI: Better Together

Human

1. Thinks with common sense
2. Has emotions and empathy
3. Can be creative and innovative

AI

1. Analyzes data and patterns
2. Has no real emotions or feelings
3. Works faster and processes large amounts of data

Real-World IT Example

Imagine a critical production application crashes during business hours. (In IT, this usually happens at the worst possible time! 😊)

AI quickly analyzes the logs and suggests two possible solutions:

Solution A: Restart the affected servers immediately and restore the application within 5 minutes.

Solution B: Perform a detailed investigation, which may take 30 minutes, but ensures that no customer data is affected.

From a technical perspective, Solution A appears to be the faster choice.

However, an experienced engineer understands that protecting customer data is more important than reducing downtime by a few minutes. After evaluating the business's impact and risks, the engineer chooses Solution B.

AI can identify the available options.

Humans understand the consequences of each option.

AI is a powerful assistant, but human judgment remains essential when making critical decisions.

An experienced engineer can assess the situation, make the right decisions under pressure, coordinate with teams, and ensure the issue is resolved with minimal impact.

This highlights an important truth: AI is a powerful assistant, but it is not a replacement for human expertise.

AI knows the options. Humans choose the best option.

That is why the future is not about Human vs AI - it is about Humans and AI working together.

Don't be afraid.
Human + AI.

4
The Human Advantage

We've now gained a basic understanding of AI. I added a couple of chapters just to provide a foundational overview, because AI is a vast subject. Since this isn't a book focused on learning AI in depth, I didn't spend too much time exploring it.

After seeing AI write articles, generate code, create images, and answer questions, it is natural to wonder:

"If AI can do all this, what is left for humans?"

The answer is: **quite a lot.**

AI is powerful, but it is not human. And that makes all the difference. (Relax, humans are still needed!)

AI is powerful, but there are still important things that only humans can bring to the table.

What AI Can Do

Let's give AI the credit it deserves.

AI can:

- Process huge amounts of data
- Analyze patterns

- Generate content
- Write code
- Create images
- Summarize information
- Work 24/7
- Learn from massive datasets

In many areas, AI is faster than humans. It never gets tired. **It never asks for coffee breaks.** 😊

What AI Cannot Do

Despite its impressive capabilities, AI has limitations.

AI cannot:

- Feel emotions
- Build genuine relationships
- Understand human experiences
- Apply real-world wisdom
- Take moral responsibility
- Show empathy
- Understand context perfectly

AI knows the information. Humans understand the meaning. That is a huge difference.

Common Sense

One of the most underrated human abilities is **common sense**.

Humans naturally understand situations that aren't written down anywhere.

Example

A GPS might suggest the fastest route.

A local driver knows the road is flooded due to heavy rain and chooses another route.

AI follows the data. Humans understand reality.

(**Anyone who has blindly followed GPS into a dead-end street knows this is true!**)

Creativity

AI is excellent at improving existing ideas.

Humans are excellent at creating new ones.

AI learns from patterns, designs, and solutions that already exist.

Humans can imagine solutions that nobody has thought of before.

Leadership

AI can analyze information, identify patterns, and suggest possible solutions.

Humans make decisions, take responsibility, and inspire others to move forward.

Leadership is not about having the most information.

It is about using judgment, building trust, and guiding people through uncertainty.

AI provides insights. Leaders provide direction.

Emotions

AI can understand what you say.

Humans can understand what you feel.

Example

Imagine a company that announces a major reorganization. Employees start worrying:

"Will my role change?"

"Will my team be affected?"

"Should I start looking for another job?"

AI can answer questions about policies, processes, and organizational changes.

But AI cannot sit with a worried employee, understand their concerns, reassure them, and help them navigate uncertainty.

A good manager can. A good leader can. A good mentor can. A good colleague can.

Technology can provide information. Humans provide comfort.

And sometimes, that makes all the difference.

AI may be powerful, but let's not forget one important fact: AI was invented by humans.(*After all, the student hasn't replaced the teacher yet!)* 😁 . Every breakthrough in artificial intelligence started with human imagination, creativity, and innovation.

Don't be afraid.
Human > AI.

5
Will AI Replace My Job?

If humans still have unique advantages, then why are so many people worried about their jobs?

In this chapter, we'll tackle the biggest question of all:

"Will AI replace my job? Will it make me lose my job?"

It is a reasonable concern. Every major technological revolution has changed the way people work. The Industrial Revolution transformed manufacturing. Computers changed offices. The internet changed communication and business.

Now, AI is transforming almost every industry.

Jobs Most Likely to Change

AI is expected to automate portions of jobs rather than entire professions.

Examples include:

Customer Support

- AI chatbots can answer routine questions.

- Human agents handle complex or emotional situations.

Software Development

- AI can generate code and suggest solutions.
- Developers still design systems, solve complex problems, and make architectural decisions.

Marketing

- AI can create content and analyze trends.
- Marketers still develop strategy and brand positioning.

Finance

- AI can identify anomalies and generate forecasts.
- Financial experts interpret results and make investment decisions.

Healthcare

- AI can assist in diagnosing diseases.
- Doctors provide treatment plans and patient care.

The Real Threat Is Not AI

Many people worry that AI will replace them.

A more accurate statement is:

"AI may not replace you, but someone using AI might."

Consider two employees:

Employee A

- Works traditionally
- Completes a report in 4 hours

Employee B

- Uses AI to gather information
- Uses AI to draft the report
- Reviews and improves the output
- Completes the report in 1 hour

Both employees are skilled.

However, **Employee B** produces more value in less time.

Organizations naturally reward productivity.

Now you see what I'm trying to say. The threat isn't AI. The real competition comes from people who have already learned how to use AI effectively.

AI won't replace you, but someone who knows how to use AI might outperform you.

Don't be afraid - upgrade your skills.

When we started our IT careers, we didn't know everything. We learned new technologies, adapted to changing trends, and stayed relevant. AI is just another change in the technology landscape. We'll do what we've always done: learn, adapt, and grow.

Don't be afraid.

Upgrade your skills.

6
AI and Layoffs

By now, you might be thinking:

"If AI is supposed to help employees, why are companies laying off so many people? Why not simply train employees to use AI?"

That's a fair question.

In fact, it is one of the most common questions people ask when discussing AI.

Let's look at reality.

First, we need to understand one thing: many of us assume that AI is the reason behind these layoffs. But that's not entirely true. (**Let's not make AI the villain of every corporate story.**)

The wave of layoffs didn't start because of the AI. During the COVID period, many companies hired more employees than they actually needed. Later, they had to reduce their workforce to balance costs and adjust to changing business conditions. Economic challenges and global uncertainty made the situation worse. AI came into the picture later and sped up the changes, but it was not the main reason the layoffs began.

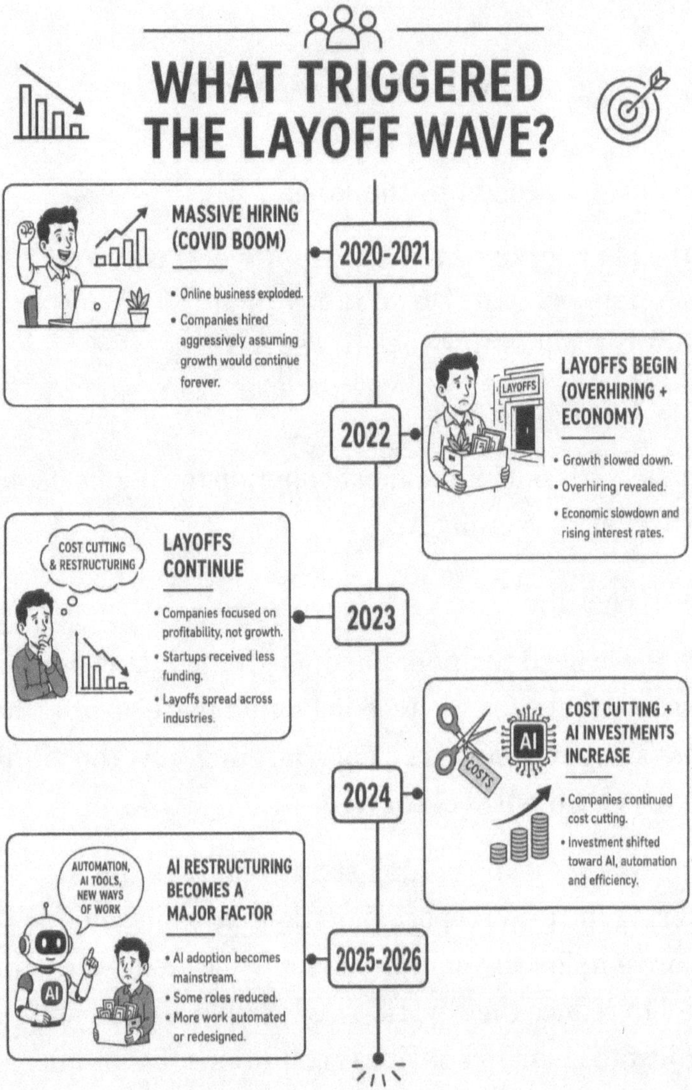

Then, Why Don't Companies Simply Train Employees?

Many companies do.

In fact, organizations around the world are investing billions of dollars in AI training and upskilling programs.

The truth is that companies have always evolved with technology. They expect employees to evolve as well.

(Technology keeps changing. Luckily, IT professionals are already experts at learning new things!)

A Difficult Truth

Technology has always increased productivity.

When tractors were introduced, farms needed fewer workers.

When computers arrived, many manual tasks disappeared.

When the Internet became mainstream, some traditional businesses struggled while entirely new industries emerged.

AI is following the same pattern.

Some roles will shrink. Some roles will evolve. Some entirely new roles will appear.

The Real Question

Instead of worrying,

"Will AI replace me?"

Ask yourself:

"How can I learn AI and stay ahead?"

Because the future belongs to those who adapt, not those who resist change.

Example

Imagine two software engineers.

One continues working the old way.

The other uses AI to code, test, learn, and work faster.

A year later, who is more productive?

As mentioned earlier, the future is not **Human vs. AI**. It is **Human vs. Human + AI**.

What Companies Really Want

Most companies are not looking for fewer people.

They are looking for:

- Higher productivity
- Faster delivery
- Better quality
- Lower costs
- More innovation

Employees who learn AI can help achieve those goals.

That makes them more valuable, not less.

Many of us have concerns and questions about layoffs. Let's take a moment to separate fear from reality and understand what's actually happening.

Fear vs Reality

1. Fear: "Companies are firing people because AI is replacing everyone."

Reality: Companies are adapting to new technologies, economic conditions, and changing business needs.

2. Fear: "There will be no jobs left."

Reality: There will be different jobs, new skills, and new opportunities.

3. Fear: "I'm too late."

Reality: We are still in the early stages of the AI revolution.

Don't be afraid.
Learn AI. Stay Ahead.

7
How to Start Learning AI

By now, you might be thinking:

"Okay, I understand AI."

"I know it's important."

"I know I shouldn't be afraid of it."

"But how do I actually learn AI?"

When we talk about learning AI, we can divide it into two paths:

Using AI – Learning how to use AI tools like ChatGPT, Gemini, and Claude effectively.

Building AI – Learning how AI models are created, trained, and deployed.

For most people, learning how to use AI is enough. Building AI is mainly for those pursuing AI-related careers.

Choose the path that matches your goals - but remember, every AI journey starts with curiosity.

(Like it or not, we have to pick one of these paths. Sitting on the fence isn't a long-term strategy - especially when AI is running at full speed! 😄)

Path 1: Learning How to use AI

This is the path most people need.

- Students.
- Teachers.
- Managers.
- Developers.
- Business owners.
- Healthcare professionals.
- Content creators.

Almost everyone can benefit from AI without learning programming.

Start learning AI with popular tools such as:

- ChatGPT
- Gemini
- Claude
- Copilot
- Perplexity

Don't try to learn all of them at once. Pick one and start using it.

There are numerous AI tools available today (**I have listed a few popular AI tools in the "Popular AI Tools" section at the end of the book**). It's not practical to learn all of them, so let's begin with a few widely used tools and develop a solid understanding of them.

Path 2: Learning How to Build AI

This path is for people who want to:

- Become AI Engineers
- Become Machine Learning Engineers
- Build AI applications
- Create AI products
- Work in AI development

If your goal is simply to use AI effectively, you can skip this section for now.

What Should You Learn?

I have included a list of AI careers and explained each role, its key responsibilities, required skills, and technology stack in the "**AI Careers Explained**" section at the end of the book.

Programming

The first step is learning a programming language.

The most popular language for AI is: **Python**

Python is widely used because it is simple, powerful, and has a large AI ecosystem. (Python was created in 1991. Python was quietly doing its job for years. Then AI arrived and suddenly turned it into a celebrity!).

Machine Learning (ML)

Machine Learning teaches computers to learn from experience (data) and make predictions or decisions on their own.

You'll learn concepts such as:

- Classification
- Regression
- Prediction
- Pattern Recognition

Deep Learning

Deep Learning is a branch of Machine Learning that uses artificial neural networks inspired by the human brain to learn from large amounts of data.

Topics include:

- Neural Networks
- Computer Vision
- Natural Language Processing

Data

AI learns from data. Understanding data is extremely important.

Learn:

- Data Collection
- Data Cleaning
- Data Analysis
- Data Visualization

Generative AI

Generative AI is a type of Artificial Intelligence that can create new content such as text, images, music, videos, and code based on patterns learned from existing data.

Topics include:

- Large Language Models (LLMs)
- Transformers
- Prompt Engineering
- RAG
- Vector Databases

AI Frameworks

AI frameworks provide tools and libraries that help developers build, train, and deploy AI applications efficiently.

• TensorFlow • PyTorch • LangChain • LangGraph • Hugging Face • Transformers • LlamaIndex • CrewAI • AutoGen • DSPy • OpenCV	• Scikit-learn • MLflow • ONNX Runtime • Haystack • Semantic Kernel • PydanticAI • Agno • Flowise • Dify • Ollama

The AI ecosystem is evolving rapidly, with thousands of frameworks, tools, and platforms available today. The frameworks listed here are some of the most popular and widely adopted in the AI community.

These tools help developers build AI-powered applications.

Cloud Platforms

Many AI applications run on cloud platforms.

Examples:

- AWS
- Azure
- Google Cloud

Which Path Should You Choose?

If your goal is:

- Better productivity
- Career growth
- Learning faster
- Staying relevant

Choose: **Using AI**

If your goal is:

- Building AI products
- Becoming an AI Engineer
- Creating AI applications

Choose: **Building AI**

There is no right or wrong choice. Both paths are valuable.

Don't be afraid.

Learn AI. Grow Faster.

8
AI Careers and Opportunities

"What opportunities will AI create?"

Whenever a major technology becomes mainstream, an entire ecosystem of new jobs emerges around it.

For example:

Internet: Web Developers, SEO Experts, Digital Marketers
Cloud: Cloud Engineers, DevOps Engineers, Cloud Architects
Mobile: App Developers, UX Designers, Mobile Architects

Similarly, AI is creating many new career opportunities.

As I mentioned before, today, AI is being adopted across almost every industry:

- Education
- Healthcare
- Banking
- Manufacturing
- Retail

- Marketing
- Human Resources
- Customer Support
- Software Development

AI-Related Jobs Emerging Today

Every technology revolution creates new jobs, and AI is no exception. Some of today's hottest AI careers didn't exist a few years ago, and many future roles are still waiting to be invented. The future job market might be writing its job descriptions as we speak!

Technical Roles

- AI Engineer
- Machine Learning Engineer
- AI Architect
- Data Scientist
- AI Researcher
- AI Platform Engineer
- MLOps Engineer
- AI Solutions Architect

Prompt Engineering Roles

- Prompt Engineer
- Prompt Designer
- Prompt Architect
- AI Conversation Designer
- AI Workflow Engineer

AI Security Roles

- AI Security Engineer
- AI Security Specialist
- AI Security Architect
- AI Privacy Specialist
- AI Red Team Engineer
- AI Trust & Safety Specialist

AI Business & Strategy Roles

- AI Product Manager
- AI Consultant
- AI Program Manager
- AI Strategy Consultant
- AI Adoption Specialist

Content & Creative Roles

- AI Content Creator
- AI Video Creator
- AI Graphic Designer
- AI Marketing Specialist
- AI Copywriter

Training & Education Roles

- AI Trainer
- AI Instructor
- AI Curriculum Designer
- AI Coach
- AI Learning Consultant

Operations & Governance Roles

- AI Governance Specialist
- AI Compliance Officer
- Responsible AI Specialist
- AI Risk Analyst
- AI Auditor

If you would like to learn more about these technical roles in detail, I have included a brief description of each role in **the chapter** titled **'AI Careers Explained'** at the end of the book.

Building AI is only one part of the AI ecosystem. As AI adoption grows, opportunities are emerging in prompting, security, governance, automation, education, consulting, and many other areas.

Prompt Engineering

Prompt Engineering is the skill of asking AI the right questions and giving clear instructions to get better results. The more specific and detailed your prompt is, the more accurate and useful the AI's response will be. As AI becomes a part of everyday work, Prompt Engineering is becoming one of the most valuable skills because the same AI tool can produce very different results depending on how it is instructed.

Example of Prompt Engineering

Imagine two people using the same AI tool.

Person 1 asks:

"Teach me AI."

Person 2 asks:

"Teach me AI from the basics. Create a 30-day learning plan for a beginner with no technical background. Spend 30 minutes per day and include free resources."

Who will get the better answer?

Obviously, Person 2.

The AI is the same. The difference is the prompt.

That's why Prompt Engineering is becoming one of the most valuable skills in the AI era.

I hope you now understand why Prompt Engineering is so important.

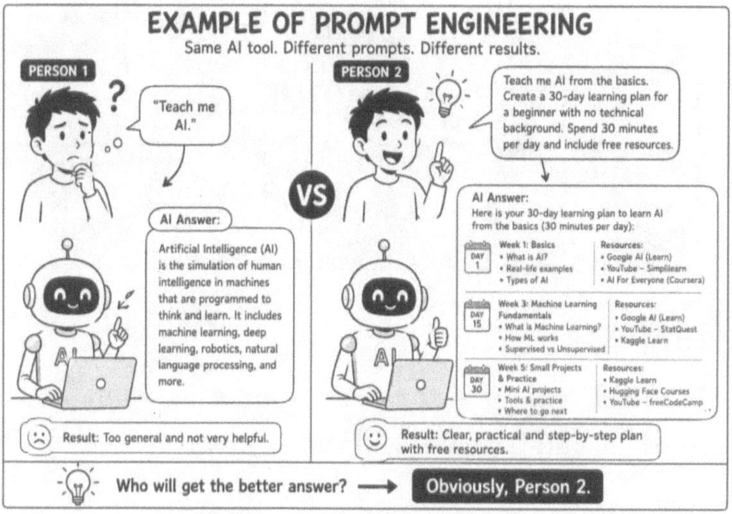

Bad Prompt = Generic Answer

Good Prompt = Better Answer

Great Prompt = Great Answer

Opportunities for Non-IT Professionals

You don't need to become a programmer to benefit from AI.

"AI is not just for engineers. It's for everyone."

The best part? AI speaks plain English much better than it speaks complicated code!

Teachers

AI can help create lesson plans, quizzes, learning materials, and personalized learning experiences.

Students

AI can help with learning, research, exam preparation, and skill development.

Business Owners

AI can assist with marketing, customer support, content creation, and business planning.

HR Professionals

AI can help screen resumes, schedule interviews, and improve employee experiences.

Marketing Professionals

AI can generate content, analyze customer behavior, and improve campaign performance.

AI is not limited to technology professionals.

It is becoming a valuable tool for everyone.

Don't spend your time worrying about what might disappear. Focus on the opportunities that are being created.

Our responsibility is not to fear change, but to recognize the opportunities it brings, align them with our skills and interests, and prepare ourselves to succeed in the future.

Technology has always changed the way we work. Those who spend less time worrying and more time learning usually end up writing the next success story.

Don't be afraid.
Opportunity is everywhere.

9
The Future of AI

Nobody can predict the future perfectly.

But if current trends continue, the next five years could be one of the most exciting periods in technology history.

AI Will Become Part of Everyday Work

(Just like Wi-Fi, we'll probably stop noticing AI - until it stops working!)

Today, AI is a tool that many people use occasionally.

By 2030, AI may become as common as email, smartphones, and the Internet. Many organizations are already moving from AI experimentation to large-scale deployment.

Where Is AI Heading Next?

AI has evolved rapidly over the past few decades. It started with simple rule-based systems, evolved into Machine Learning and Deep Learning, and today we are living in the era of Generative AI.

But the AI journey is far from over.

Generative AI (Today)

Today's AI can create content such as text, images, videos, music, and software code. Tools like ChatGPT, Claude, Gemini, and Midjourney have already transformed the way people work, learn, and create.

(A few years ago, asking a computer to write a poem sounded strange. Today, it sounds normal. The future will probably surprise us even more)

Agentic AI (Emerging)

The next stage of AI is Agentic AI. Instead of simply answering questions, AI will be able to perform tasks on behalf of users. It may schedule meetings, manage workflows, book travel, conduct research, and complete multi-step activities with minimal human intervention.

Artificial General Intelligence (AGI)

Many researchers believe the long-term goal of AI is Artificial General Intelligence (AGI). AGI would be capable of learning, reasoning, and solving problems across many domains, much like humans do today. Unlike current AI systems, it would not be limited to specific tasks. **For now, AGI is still a topic for researchers. So don't panic.**

Artificial Super Intelligence (ASI)

Beyond AGI lies the theoretical concept of Artificial Super Intelligence (ASI), where AI could surpass human intelligence in many areas. While ASI remains a topic of research and discussion, it does not exist today. **Fortunately, ASI doesn't exist today. Most of us are still trying to remember all our passwords.**

AI Adoption by Organizations

AI adoption has grown dramatically over the last decade. According to industry surveys, only about **20% of organizations were using AI in 2017**. By **2024, adoption had risen to over 70%**, and by **2025 it was approaching 80%**. Some industry reports suggest that **AI adoption could reach nearly 90% by 2026**, making AI one of the fastest-adopted technologies in business history.

What the Future May Look Like by 2030

Industry forecasts suggest that AI will become a core part of business operations across almost every industry by 2030. Most professionals are expected to work alongside AI, with many routine tasks being automated. AI is projected to contribute trillions of dollars to the global economy, while organizations continue investing heavily in AI technologies.

AI agents and intelligent assistants are also expected to become increasingly common, helping businesses improve productivity and efficiency.

AI and Cybersecurity

AI runs on data, and much of that data can be very valuable. As AI becomes a bigger part of our lives and businesses, protecting that data will become increasingly important. Building powerful AI systems is only part of the challenge - keeping them secure is equally important.

As AI grows, cyber threats will grow too. Hackers will continue looking for new ways to attack systems and steal information. This means cybersecurity will become more important than ever, creating many new opportunities for security professionals. **After all, the smarter AI becomes, the smarter the people protecting it will need to be.**

Regardless of how AI evolves, the most realistic future is not Human vs AI.

It is **Human + AI**.

Together, they can achieve more than either could alone.

Don't be afraid.
Choose your future.

The previous two pages are intentionally left blank.

Not because this book has run out of words.

But because your mind deserves a moment of silence.

Forget everything you've heard about AI for just a moment.

Forget fear. Forget the hype. Forget the noise.

Take a deep breath. Relax.

Clear your mind. Leave your fears behind.

The future is not something to fear.

It's something to prepare for.

Ready? Let's move to the final chapter.

10

Don't Be Afraid. Win with AI

We've finally reached the end of the chapter.

I hope this book has helped remove at least some of your fears about AI.

As I mentioned earlier, fear is often the biggest thing that stops us from trying something new.

Fear starts to lose its power the moment we face it.

When we were children, we never worried about how difficult learning would be. We simply learned.

Maybe that's the mindset we need again.

Less fear. More curiosity.

Less worrying. More learning.

And if there's one message I'd like you to remember after closing this book, it's this:

Don't let fear decide your future.

Let learning decide it. Let curiosity decide it. Let action decide it.

One thing I've learned throughout my career is that change is inevitable.

Technology changes.

Industries change.

Skills change.

The world changes.

The people who succeed are rarely the ones who resist change.

They are the ones who learn how to adapt to it.

As I mentioned in the previous chapter, a few years from now, AI will be more powerful than it is today.

The question is:

Where will you be? Will you be watching the future? Or will you be part of it?

Keep learning. Keep growing. Keep believing in yourself.

Because your future is not decided by AI.

It's decided by the choices you make today.

The best time to start is now.

Thank you.

And all the very best for your future.

Don't Be Afraid.

Win with AI.

AI Dictionary

Essential AI Terms Everyone Should Know

Artificial Intelligence is transforming the way we live, learn, and work. Along the way, you've probably come across many AI-related words and technical terms.

Don't worry—you don't need to memorize them all. This section provides simple, one-line explanations of the most important AI terms to help you understand and confidently navigate the world of AI.

Must-Know AI Terms

1. AI (Artificial Intelligence)

Technology that enables machines to perform tasks that normally require human intelligence.

2. Machine Learning (ML)

A branch of AI that learns data and improves without explicit programming.

3. Deep Learning

An advanced form of Machine Learning that uses neural networks to solve complex problems.

4. Neural Network

A system inspired by the human brain that helps AI recognize patterns and make decisions.

5. Generative AI (GenAI)

AI that creates new content such as text, images, music, videos, and code.

6. Agentic AI

AI that can plan, make decisions, and perform tasks with minimal human intervention.

7. LLM (Large Language Model)

A powerful AI model trained in large amounts of text to understand and generate language.

8. Prompt

The instruction or question given to an AI system.

9. Prompt Engineering

The skill of writing effective prompts to get better AI results.

10. AI Agent

An AI system designed to perform tasks and achieve specific goals autonomously.

11. Training

The process of teaching an AI model using large amounts of data.

12. Fine-Tuning

Additional training that specializes in an AI model for specific tasks.

13. Dataset

A collection of data used to train and evaluate AI models.

14. Token

A small unit of text processed by an AI model.

15. Context Window

The amount of information an AI can consider at one time.

16. Embedding

A numerical representation of information that helps AI understand the meaning.

17. Inference

The process of generating answers or predictions using a trained AI model.

18. Hallucination

When AI generates information that sounds correct but is actually wrong.

19. Bias

Unfair or inaccurate results caused by limitations in training data.

20. Ethics

Principles that guide the responsible development and use of AI.

21. AI Governance

Policies and controls used to manage AI responsibly.

22. Privacy

Protecting personal and sensitive information from misuse.

23. Responsible AI

The practice of developing AI that is safe, fair, and trustworthy.

24. NLP (Natural Language Processing)

AI technology that helps computers understand human language.

25. Computer Vision

AI that enables machines to understand and analyze images and videos.

26. Speech Recognition

Technology that converts spoken language into text.

27. Text-to-Speech (TTS)

Technology that converts text into spoken audio.

28. Text-to-Image

AI technology that creates images from written descriptions.

29. Text-to-Video

AI technology that generates videos from text prompts.

30. Semantic Search

Search based on meaning and context rather than exact keywords.

31. API (Application Programming Interface)

A way for different software applications to communicate with each other.

32. RAG (Retrieval-Augmented Generation)

A technique that lets AI retrieve information before generating responses.

33. Vector Database

A database designed to store and search for AI embeddings efficiently.

34. Open-Source AI

AI software whose source code is publicly available.

35. Multimodal AI

AI that can understand and work with text, images, audio, and video.

36. Reinforcement Learning

A learning method where AI improves through rewards and feedback.

37. Supervised Learning

Machine Learning using labeled training data.

38. Unsupervised Learning

Machine Learning that finds patterns without labeled examples.

39. AGI (Artificial General Intelligence)

A future AI capable of performing most intellectual tasks a human can do.

40. ASI (Artificial Super Intelligence)

A theoretical AI that surpasses human intelligence.

41. Digital Twin – A virtual representation of a real-world object, system, or process.

42. Autonomous Agent

An AI system that can perform tasks independently.

43. AI Workflow

A sequence of AI-driven steps used to automate a process.

44. AI Automation – Using AI to automate repetitive or complex tasks.

45. Agentic Workflow

A workflow where AI agents perform and coordinate multiple tasks.

46. AI Orchestration

Managing multiple AI systems and workflows together.

47. MCP (Model Context Protocol)

A standard that helps AI models connect with external tools and data sources.

48. AI Copilot

An AI assistant that works alongside humans to improve productivity.

49. AI Assistant

An AI-powered helper that supports users with various tasks.

50. AI Companion

An AI designed for ongoing interaction, assistance, and conversation.

51. Synthetic Data

Artificially generated data used for training AI models.

52. Foundation Model

A large AI model that can be adapted for many different tasks.

53. AI Reasoning

The ability of AI to analyze information and make logical conclusions.

54. AI Alignment

Ensuring AI systems behave according to human goals and values.

55. GPU (Graphics Processing Unit)

A specialized processor that accelerates AI training and computation.

56. Transformer Model

The AI architecture behind modern systems such as ChatGPT and Gemini.

57. Quantization

A technique that reduces AI model size and improves efficiency.

58. Knowledge Base

A structured collection of information used by AI systems.

59. Vector Search

A method of finding similar information using embeddings.

60. Retrieval System

A system that finds relevant information before AI generates responses.

61. AI Guardrails

Safety mechanisms that help prevent harmful AI behavior.

62. AI Safety

The field focused on making AI secure and beneficial.

63. Human-in-the-Loop

A process where humans review, guide, or approve AI decisions.

64. AI Agent: An AI-powered system that can think, decide, and perform tasks automatically to achieve a goal with minimal human input.

65. Embeddings: A way for AI to convert words or data into numbers so it can understand meaning and find similar information.

(AI is a massive and ever-growing field. The words I've mentioned are just the tip of the iceberg - or perhaps more accurately, a single drop in an endless ocean.)

Popular AI Tools

AI Assistants

- ChatGPT
- Gemini
- Claude
- Copilot
- Perplexity

AI Coding

- GitHub Copilot
- Cursor
- Windsurf
- Claude Code
- Aider

AI Image Generation

- Midjourney
- DALL·E
- Adobe Firefly
- Stable Diffusion
- Ideogram

AI Video Generation

- Sora
- Runway
- Veo
- Pika
- Synthesia

AI Automation & Agents

- n8n
- LangChain
- LangGraph
- CrewAI
- AutoGen

AI Productivity

- Notion AI
- Canva AI
- Gamma
- Tome
- Beautiful.ai

AI Development Platforms

- OpenAI
- Anthropic
- Google AI

- Azure AI
- AWS Bedrock

Today, tens of thousands of AI tools are available worldwide, and new tools are being launched almost every day. The challenge is no longer finding an AI tool - the challenge is choosing the right one.

(By the time you finish reading this chapter, someone has probably launched three new AI tools!)

AI Careers Explained

I gathered this information by searching through a few AI tools. Some of the careers and key skills may vary slightly from one source to another.

As I said earlier, AI is a tool that helps us grow. AI tools greatly assisted me in writing this book. Instead of being afraid of AI, we should explore the roles that suit us, learn the necessary skills, and begin our AI journey. The future belongs to those who learn and adapt.

Technical Roles

Data Scientist

- **Definition:** Analyzes large datasets, identifies patterns, and drives data-driven decisions.
- **Key Skills:** Python, SQL, Statistics, Machine Learning, Data Visualization
- **Tech Stack:** Jupyter, Pandas, NumPy, SciPy, Matplotlib, Seaborn, Tableau, Power BI, Spark

Machine Learning Engineer

- **Definition:** Builds, trains, tests, and deploys ML models.

- **Key Skills:** Python, Scikit-learn, TensorFlow, PyTorch, MLOps
- **Tech Stack:** MLflow, DVC, Airflow, FastAPI, ONNX, Hugging Face, Docker, Kubernetes

---

AI Researcher

- **Definition:** Develops new AI algorithms and techniques.
- **Key Skills:** Deep Learning, Mathematics, PyTorch, NLP, Computer Vision
- **Tech Stack:** JAX, PyTorch Lightning, Hugging Face Transformers, OpenAI Gym, CUDA, LaTeX (for papers)

AI Engineer

- **Definition:** Creates AI-powered applications (chatbots, assistants, recommendation engines).
- **Key Skills:** Python, LLMs, LangChain, RAG, APIs, Vector Databases
- **Tech Stack:** LangChain, LlamaIndex, Pinecone, Weaviate, FAISS, OpenAI API, FastAPI, Streamlit

---

MLOps Engineer

- **Definition:** Automates deployment, monitoring, and maintenance of ML models.
- **Key Skills:** Docker, Kubernetes, MLflow, CI/CD, Cloud Platforms
- **Tech Stack:** Kubeflow, ArgoCD, Jenkins, GitHub Actions, Prometheus, Grafana, AWS SageMaker, GCP Vertex AI

AI Platform Engineer

- **Definition:** Builds and manages infrastructure for AI development.
- **Key Skills:** AWS, Azure, GCP, Kubernetes, Terraform, Python
- **Tech Stack:** Terraform, Helm, Istio, Databricks, Snowflake, Apache Kafka, cloud-native monitoring tools

---

AI Solutions Architect

- **Definition:** Designs AI solutions aligned with business goals.
- **Key Skills:** Generative AI, Cloud Computing, Solution Design
- **Tech Stack:** AWS Bedrock, Azure OpenAI, GCP Vertex AI, Hugging Face Hub, Databricks, REST/GraphQL APIs

AI Architect

- **Definition:** Defines AI vision, governance, and architecture strategy.
- **Key Skills:** AI/ML Architecture, Cloud Platforms, MLOps, Leadership
- **Tech Stack:** Enterprise AI platforms, Cloud-native orchestration, Data Lakes, Snowflake, Hadoop, Ethical AI frameworks

Prompt Engineering Roles

Prompt Engineer

- **Definition:** Designs and optimizes prompts to improve AI model outputs.
- **Key Skills:** Prompt crafting, Python, LLM APIs, Evaluation metrics
- **Tech Stack:** OpenAI API, Anthropic Claude, Hugging Face, LangChain, LlamaIndex, Jupyter

Prompt Designer

- **Definition:** Focuses on the creative and UX side of prompt creation for specific use cases.

- **Key Skills:** UX writing, Content design, NLP basics, Iterative testing
- **Tech Stack:** ChatGPT, Claude, MidJourney (for generative art), LangChain templates, Figma (for workflow design)

Prompt Architect

- **Definition:** Defines structured prompt frameworks and reusable architectures for complex AI systems.
- **Key Skills:** System design, LLM orchestration, RAG, Vector Databases
- **Tech Stack:** LangChain, LlamaIndex, Pinecone, Weaviate, FAISS, APIs, Cloud platforms (AWS/GCP/Azure)

AI Conversation Designer

- **Definition:** Designs natural, engaging conversational flows for chatbots and virtual assistants.
- **Key Skills:** Dialogue design, UX, NLP, Empathy mapping
- **Tech Stack:** Dialogflow, Rasa, Botpress, Voiceflow, Azure Bot Service, Twilio

---

AI Workflow Engineer

- **Definition:** Builds end-to-end workflows integrating AI models into business processes.
- **Key Skills:** Workflow automation, APIs, Orchestration, MLOps
- **Tech Stack:** Airflow, Prefect, LangChain, Zapier, n8n, Kubernetes, Cloud-native pipelines

---

AI Security Roles

AI Security Engineer

- **Definition:** Protects AI systems from adversarial attacks, data breaches, and misuse.
- **Key Skills:** Cybersecurity, Adversarial ML, Python, Threat Modeling
- **Tech Stack:** TensorFlow Security, PyTorch Adversarial Libraries, OWASP, Burp Suite, Wireshark, Cloud IAM

AI Security Analyst

- **Definition:** Monitors AI systems for vulnerabilities, compliance, and suspicious activity.
- **Key Skills:** Risk Assessment, Monitoring, Incident Response, Compliance

- **Tech Stack:** Splunk, ELK Stack, SIEM tools, Cloud Security tools (AWS GuardDuty, Azure Security Center)

AI Security Architect

- **Definition:** Designs secure AI architectures, ensuring governance, compliance, and resilience.
- **Key Skills:** AI/ML Architecture, Security Frameworks, Cloud Security, Leadership
- **Tech Stack:** NIST AI RMF, ISO/IEC 27001, Cloud-native security tools, Kubernetes RBAC, Terraform with security modules

AI Privacy Engineer

- **Definition:** Ensures AI systems comply with privacy laws and protect sensitive data.
- **Key Skills:** Differential Privacy, Federated Learning, Data Governance, Legal Compliance
- **Tech Stack:** TensorFlow Privacy, PySyft, Homomorphic Encryption libraries, GDPR/CCPA compliance tools

AI Red Team Specialist

- **Definition:** Simulates attacks on AI systems to identify weaknesses before adversaries exploit them.
- **Key Skills:** Adversarial Testing, Penetration Testing, Ethical Hacking, ML Security
- **Tech Stack:** CleverHans, Foolbox, Adversarial Robustness Toolbox (ART), Kali Linux, Metasploit

---

AI Governance & Compliance Officer

- **Definition:** Oversees AI ethics, regulations, and compliance with global standards.
- **Key Skills:** Policy Design, Risk Management, AI Ethics, Regulatory Knowledge
- **Tech Stack:** NIST AI RMF, EU AI Act frameworks, ISO standards, Compliance dashboards

---

AI Business & Strategy Roles

AI Product Manager

- **Definition:** Oversees the development and lifecycle of AI-powered products, ensuring they meet user needs and business goals.
- **Key Skills:** Product Strategy, Roadmapping, Stakeholder Management, AI/ML basics

- **Tech Stack:** Jira, Trello, Aha!, Productboard, Analytics tools (Mixpanel, Amplitude), Cloud AI APIs

---

AI Consultant

- **Definition:** Advises organizations on AI adoption, implementation, and optimization strategies.
- **Key Skills:** Business Analysis, AI/ML knowledge, Communication, Solution Design
- **Tech Stack:** Power BI, Tableau, Cloud AI services (AWS SageMaker, Azure AI, GCP Vertex AI), LangChain

---

AI Program Manager

- **Definition:** Manages large-scale AI initiatives, coordinating teams, budgets, and timelines.
- **Key Skills:** Program Management, Risk Management, Agile/Waterfall, AI Governance
- **Tech Stack:** MS Project, Asana, Jira, Confluence, Cloud dashboards, Compliance tools

---

AI Strategy Consultant

- **Definition:** Develops long-term AI strategies aligned with organizational vision and competitive advantage.
- **Key Skills:** Strategic Thinking, Market Analysis, AI Trends, Executive Communication
- **Tech Stack:** McKinsey-style frameworks, SWOT/PESTEL tools, Cloud AI platforms, Generative AI for scenario modeling

---

AI Adoption Specialist

- **Definition:** Drives organizational adoption of AI tools, ensuring smooth integration and user training.
- **Key Skills:** Change Management, Training, Communication, AI Tool Familiarity
- **Tech Stack:** LMS platforms (Coursera, Udemy Business), Collaboration tools (Teams, Slack), AI SaaS tools (ChatGPT Enterprise, Copilot, Notion AI)

Content & Creative Roles

AI Content Creator

- **Definition:** Produces written, visual, or multimedia content using AI tools to engage audiences.

- **Key Skills:** Content strategy, Storytelling, Generative AI, SEO basics
- **Tech Stack:** ChatGPT, Jasper, Notion AI, Canva, Copy.ai, SurferSEO

AI Video Creator

- **Definition:** Uses AI to generate, edit, and enhance video content for marketing, education, or entertainment.
- **Key Skills:** Video editing, Scriptwriting, Motion graphics, AI video generation
- **Tech Stack:** RunwayML, Synthesia, Pictory, Descript, Adobe Premiere Pro, After Effects

---

AI Graphic Designer

- **Definition:** Creates visual designs, illustrations, and branding assets using AI-powered tools.
- **Key Skills:** Design principles, Creativity, Generative art, Branding
- **Tech Stack:** MidJourney, DALL·E, Stable Diffusion, Canva, Figma, Adobe Creative Suite

---

AI Marketing Specialist

- **Definition:** Leverages AI to design and execute marketing campaigns that drive engagement and conversions.
- **Key Skills:** Digital marketing, Analytics, Generative AI, Customer segmentation
- **Tech Stack:** HubSpot, Marketo, Salesforce Einstein, Persado, Copy.ai, Google Analytics

---

AI Copywriter

- **Definition:** Writes persuasive, engaging, and tailored copy using AI tools for ads, websites, and campaigns.
- **Key Skills:** Creative writing, Persuasion, SEO, Generative AI
- **Tech Stack:** Jasper, Copy.ai, Writesonic, ChatGPT, Grammarly, SurferSEO

Training & Education Roles

AI Trainer

- **Definition:** Teaches AI models by curating datasets, fine-tuning, and guiding model behavior.
- **Key Skills:** Data preparation, Annotation, Model fine-tuning, Evaluation

- **Tech Stack:** Label Studio, Prodigy, Hugging Face, OpenAI fine-tuning tools, Python, Jupyter

---

AI Instructor

- **Definition:** Provides structured learning experiences to teach AI concepts and tools to learners.
- **Key Skills:** Teaching, Curriculum delivery, AI/ML knowledge, Communication
- **Tech Stack:** LMS platforms (Moodle, Coursera, Udemy), Jupyter Notebooks, Google Colab, Zoom/Teams

---

AI Curriculum Designer

- **Definition:** Designs educational programs and learning paths for AI training.
- **Key Skills:** Instructional design, Pedagogy, AI/ML knowledge, Assessment design
- **Tech Stack:** Articulate 360, Canvas LMS, Figma (for course design), Generative AI tools for content creation

---

AI Coach

- **Definition:** Provides personalized guidance to learners or professionals adopting AI tools.
- **Key Skills:** Mentorship, Communication, Applied AI knowledge, Problem-solving
- **Tech Stack:** Mentoring platforms, Collaboration tools (Slack, Teams), AI SaaS tools (ChatGPT Enterprise, Copilot)

AI Learning Consultant

- **Definition:** Advises organizations on AI learning strategies and workforce upskilling.
- **Key Skills:** Learning strategy, Change management, AI/ML knowledge, Stakeholder engagement
- **Tech Stack:** LMS analytics, Power BI, Tableau, AI training platforms, Cloud AI services

---

Operations & Governance Roles

AI Governance Specialist

- **Definition:** Establishes governance frameworks to ensure responsible AI use.
- **Key Skills:** Policy design, Risk management, AI ethics, Compliance frameworks

- **Tech Stack:** NIST AI RMF, EU AI Act tools, ISO standards, Governance dashboards

---

AI Compliance Officer

- **Definition:** Ensures AI systems comply with regulatory and legal requirements.
- **Key Skills:** Regulatory knowledge, Risk assessment, Documentation, Auditing
- **Tech Stack:** GDPR/CCPA compliance tools, ISO/IEC 27001, Cloud compliance dashboards

---

Responsible AI Specialist

- **Definition:** Focuses on ethical AI practices, fairness, transparency, and accountability.
- **Key Skills:** AI ethics, Bias detection, Transparency frameworks, Stakeholder communication
- **Tech Stack:** Fairlearn, AIF360, Explainable AI tools (SHAP, LIME), Ethical AI frameworks

---

AI Risk Analyst

- **Definition:** Identifies and evaluates risks associated with AI adoption and deployment.
- **Key Skills:** Risk modeling, Threat analysis, AI/ML knowledge, Scenario planning

- **Tech Stack:** Risk dashboards, Monte Carlo simulation tools, Cloud AI monitoring, SIEM platforms

---

AI Auditor

- **Definition:** Conducts audits of AI systems to ensure compliance, fairness, and reliability.
- **Key Skills:** Auditing, Documentation, AI/ML evaluation, Regulatory knowledge
- **Tech Stack:** Audit management tools, Compliance dashboards, Explainable AI frameworks, ISO standards

www.ingramcontent.com/pod-product-compliance
Lightning Source LLC
La Vergne TN
LVHW090329210926
848480LV00004B/1352
* 9 7 9 8 9 0 5 6 0 8 8 5 8 *